THE BEST BREAKUP LINE I EVER GOT

A Young Widow's Journey to Find Love Again

TERESA SCHACHTEL

The Best Breakup Line I Ever Got
A Young Widow's Journey to Find Love Again

Teresa Schachtel

Cover art, illustration edits,
and author photo by: Shellie Dial

Character illustrations by: Teresa Schachtel

Editing and proofreading by:
Ki & C, www.kiandc.com

Dedication

This book is dedicated to my son, Zander.
May your future be bright and filled with
positive life lessons!

Special Thanks

Thank you to Christine, Kiersten, Jacque, and Zander for all
of your support and help.

And thank you to my angel of a mother, Bea,
for loving me and always making sure I
"invest in myself."

PREFACE

Within a year, I lost the two most important men in my life—the one I grew up with, and the one I married.

My dad raised me with his own hard-working hands. There I sat holding his hands as they went from warm to cold the day he died from a heart attack. I felt all the life drain out of his body at that moment. The once vibrant, intelligent, and husky, strong man I had known my whole life had now become limp and lifeless.

He had taught me how to weld with those hands, how to make model cars and airplanes, how to pitch a tent, how to wash dishes, and how to play guitar. His hands loved me unconditionally and now it was time to let them go.

The day of his funeral, it actually rained sideways. I had never seen rain like that before. And I knew every time that rain slapped me in the face, like his death, it was something I never wanted to be slapped with again.

Trip of a Lifetime

CIAO ITALIA!

Have you ever dreamt of going on a beautiful Italian vacation? Art, pizza, gelato, history, cobblestone streets, and ancient ghosts? It seemed it would always be a dream for me until it actually came true. About a year after my father died, my mom had saved up a bit of his life insurance money to travel. Dad had a heart attack at 62 and Mom had spent the past few years as his sole caretaker. Her grief—although saddening—was kind of a relief for her. This trip would be a reprieve and a gift from her husband of 45 years. And she wanted to take me!

I couldn't wait to have my fill of museums, art, and history. We would retrace the streets of our Italian heritage in Calabria at the tip of the boot. To be by my Mom's side as we visited the small village my Grandma had grown up in before immigrating to San Francisco would be life-changing. It would inspire us and be a fun mother-daughter bonding experience.

When it all came about, my husband Dean urged me to take the invitation. "Yes! Go for it, Baby! Have a great time with her. We'll go to Hawaii together next year!"

Hawaii had always been a dream of ours. Dean had been a big fan of *The Brady Bunch* and idealized the thought of us having the perfect "Brady" vacation—complete with hula dancers, kayaking, surf lessons, pineapple factory tours, and volcano hikes. It meant a lot to him and would have been his first time there.

The last time I had been to Hawaii was in my mid-twenties with my best friend from high school. She ended up meeting a guy at a palapa bar on our first night. After only an hour of piña coladas, an instantaneous lustful attraction emerged and they spent the entire vacation indoors sexing it up while I ended up swimming with dolphins by myself. Needless to say, I was looking forward to going back with my husband for a romantic "me and he" vacation. It meant a lot that he was willing to put our plans on hold another year so I could take this trip with Mom.

A few months of planning had passed and Italy was calling. I bought a translation book and furiously tried to learn common Italian phrases so I could make it to *il bagno* and order every type of tiramisu that I could possibly try. The trip finally came, and suddenly, as I stepped off the plane, I was bathing under the Tuscan sun. As an artist, I thought I might gain my soul's inspiration and heal a bit after losing Dad. To live this experience was far outside my normal grind.

I couldn't wait to take in the grandeur of something new, a place I had only studied about in my high school history books. My love for history is huge. Want to invite me to a civil war reenactment? Yes! I'll be there; and I'm dressing up in a big Southern Belle ball gown! Walking the historical streets, getting those ghostly chills at the Coliseum, and grazing with my own hands the cracks and crevices of the ruins at the Roman Forum—with all of its now uncovered statuary and hidden brothels—was astounding. These were the places my ancestors had traipsed.

Strolling through narrow, windy streets, drinking cappuccinos, breathing the salty Mediterranean air, and taking in the gorgeous landscapes, vineyards, rivers, art, and landmarks put me in a state of utter awe. There was one moment in Florence when I turned the corner in the museum of the Galleria dell'Accademia to see Michelangelo's David; my jaw actually dropped open. To think he carved one block of marble into that intricate and massive masterpiece! He depicted such a strong warrior with the most delicate veins and details in his hands.

I had received a scholarship to art school in my early college years, and we had spent time sketching and painting the "David" and other nude Italian subjects. To see the real thing was cathartic and brought everything to life. The way

Michelangelo carved each detail—down to David's finger-nails and toes—was stunning. I felt honored there, like I was among the elite to be able to experience such beloved inter-national masterpieces.

Italy was straight from the movies for this local Los Angeles girl, and the rich purples and yellows from the Tuscan sunsets have since been emblazoned in my mind as the most mag-nificent I've ever seen since.

To be here with my mom was particularly special. She had always wanted to go on a trip like this with her own mom, but it wasn't possible. Mom didn't have her mother around going into adulthood, which made this mother-daughter trip extra meaningful.

Our plan was to spend the first seven days of our trip on the typical tourist sites and then spend the second leg of the trip visiting the small village Grandma Lena was from. We would see the house she grew up in, the town she spent her childhood in, and fill our hearts with nostalgia and lineage.

After the seventh day of filling up on homemade gnoc-chi and snapping pictures of every Ferrari I spotted, I found myself in the middle of San Marco Square in Venice where they filmed *Twilight*. I pictured Edward and Bella canoodling through the dark alleys. Their pale vampiric melancholy love was all I could think about under the gothic sky that night.

My heart was filled with a longing for dark romance and filled my lifelong obsession with the macabre. This was one of the oldest and most beautiful places I had ever been to.

I texted Dean beneath a beautiful night sky, looking up at the spooky moon and crisp deep blue air. "Wish you were here," I sent, indulging in a hazelnut-filled crepe.

With orchestral violin music swelling in my ears and a cappuccino hot on my lips, my phone began to ring. It was my 11-year-old son. I couldn't wait to hear how his school carnival went the night before and how Daddy had probably won him a goldfish or some huge auction item.

But instead, these words fell from his precious little lips, "Mommy... Daddy wasn't breathing so I had to call 911." He then handed the phone to a paramedic who fumbled through a series of questions, causing me to become increasingly confused until I finally heard the words "cardiac arrest" and "I'm sorry, ma'am, but your husband has passed away."

Huh?

My hand lost its ability and the cappuccino cup slipped away, shattering into a few chunky pieces on the cobblestone below. My face went pale, my mouth dropped open, and I fell to one knee. A crowd formed around me as someone grabbed a chair for me to sit in. My Mom gazed across at me and could see something wasn't right. She ran to my side. I looked up at her with tears in my eyes and a horrified expression on my face. "My husband is dead."

I've replayed it in my head so many times that it now seems like I'm watching a movie. I look back and see myself as a ghost in that moment, like it wasn't real. I went through the motions that were all so real—getting a flight home, wondering what it would look like to walk through the front door without Dean there, and worrying what I'd be facing the rest of my life—all while floating along as a mere apparition still in denial.

You get married to do life—not death—together. When a life is taken away and you're thrust into everything alone, it's devastating and shocking. I never fathomed I'd be dealt this hand of cards at 40 years old. I scurried to change every plan so I could cut my trip short and rush home to be with my son. My plane landed in LAX. My husband didn't pick me up from the airport. I didn't get a kiss hello or a "How was your trip?" Instead, I merely walked into a dark and lonely house knowing that the fabric of my life would now be forever changed.

THEY MEET...

had just ended a relationship with a man who had been cheating on me. I was 27 and just beginning to think about getting married, maybe having kids, and pursuing my career in ophthalmology. As the heartache from my breakup faded, I met my soon-to-be husband, sipping on a blonde pale ale at a local brewhouse in Los Angeles.

Dean was on the board of a cystic fibrosis charity organization and they were having their annual music event. Rascal Flatts was the headliner in an intimate setting that night, and I was excited to let my hair down and hang out with my girlfriends. We were a gaggle of 20-something girls giggling, drinking, and singing along at a high-top bar table when I saw him.

He looked exhausted, like he'd been working all day. He wore a silver bracelet and a silky shirt with a dragon on it. To be honest, I thought it was a bit sleazy. He was a typical music producer type with graying hair. I had just come from a man who wore Dockers and polo shirts and had been the quarterback of his football team. This dragon-shirt-wearing, older man was totally not my type. With the crowd thick and no place to sit, he swayed back and forth to the music.

"This seat isn't taken if you'd like to rest your feet," I offered. We talked through the event as he dazzled me with his music knowledge. I was impressed that he had helped coordinate the event as it was turning out to be a major success. As the night drew to a close, he walked me to my car, hugged me, and asked for my email address. Not even my phone number—my email.

The next day, in my inbox was a picture of him and Billy Idol sneering, which made me chuckle. His message said, "I really enjoyed meeting you. Would you like to have dinner this weekend?" I didn't know it at the time, but it was the start of right where I wanted to be.

The date came and he picked me up at my parent's door in a fuzzy leopard print bowling shirt and jeans. I looked at my Mom and said, "No way!"

She assured me that I needed to give him a chance. It was just a shirt.

With our love of music in common, we connected quickly. I couldn't even begin to imagine the ride I would go on with him; I was merely falling in love. I remember once walking into his high-rise office at Warner Bros. Music. The halls were laden with gold records and celebrity photos. Growing up with Sebastian Bach as my first rockstar love, I was definitely starstruck and quickly admired his position.

He was genuine and charismatic. I already knew I always fell in love with the loudest guy and biggest personality in the room—and that was Dean. He was a pursuer and a communicator with the biggest, most compassionate heart I had ever seen. He had this particular way of making everyone feel special and like a valued individual.

One time a friend of his who was in a wheelchair admired his rare band t-shirt.

"They don't even make those anymore," the guy said.

As they reminisced about the band, Dean took off his shirt and gave it to his friend. I couldn't believe I'd met a man who would literally give someone the shirt off his back.

One time Dean cleaned out his closet and gave all his cargo shorts and vintage band t-shirts to the mentally ill adults who lived in a state facility in our town. From that point forward it was common for us to see them walking around town with Lamb of God and Black Sabbath t-shirts on. That was the kind of person Dean was. He put others before himself, and I was in love.

Dean was passionate about his job and later became an executive for "Dio and Motorhead" and many other bands. He seemed to literally know everyone. And for me—a young, naïve woman just beginning a career in ophthalmology—he was larger than life!

On one particular surprise first dates, Dean blindfolded me. He didn't let me know where we were going, but I suspected all the turns up to the Universal Amphitheater before it became Harry Potter World. We drove up to a private entrance, he removed the blindfold, and a tear dropped from my eye. My queen, Mariah Carey, was performing there that night, and he had "made it happen." He had arranged for us to see Mariah front row in concert. While we were backstage a woman in slick black leather cop lingerie, high heels, a short blonde wig, and fishnets called his name. "Hey, Dean-o!"

How in the hell does he know her? I thought. She was a female wrestler named Hollywood. He knew everyone from random female strippers and wrestlers to big-name music stars. It was then I started to feel smitten in admiration and eventually started to fall in love. He was like a king in the music industry. I looked up to him.

Like I said, he knew everyone. Even people I would never expect. As we dated, he continued to incorporate me into his life. I never imagined I'd be having a conversation with Alice Cooper about his parents who had been married for 75 years, or that I'd hear Keith Urban call me "sweetheart."

After all the times I'd sung along to Alanis Morissette's songs and looked up to her, I now found myself eating grapes and cheese backstage with her. We got to go on the tour bus just to say hi to Dwight Yoakam and Alan Jackson. We partied backstage with Kid Rock, Marilyn Manson, and I even had conversations with Connie Francis about her life as a small-town Italian girl who grew up in a Jewish neighborhood. Everyone expressed their gratitude to Dean for working on their albums and making them feel special.

The lifestyle was exciting and opened my eyes to a new way of life. Six months later, we were having dinner at Miceli's Italian restaurant as Kenny Rogers walked in. I couldn't believe the way my life had taken such a bizarre—but wonderful—turn. All of a sudden, an opera singer started singing, "A Whole New World" from Aladdin. In the middle of the restaurant, Dean made my dreams come true that night as a bottle of champagne was popped and he got down on one knee. I said, "Yes!" and cried as he slipped an engagement ring on my finger. I stroked his fuzzy leopard shirt and knew he had just offered me "the fairytale."

We spent the next six months planning our wedding and were married within a year of meeting—and I never once had cold feet or second thoughts. I remember walking down the aisle, staring at him standing at the altar. He looked back over his shoulder and I knew. I knew by the peacefulness in his smile—the way that it calmed me and made me feel secure—that this was the right decision. My dad whispered, "Are you nervous?" and I answered with every truthful bone in my body, "No. Not one bit."

THE FANTASY ENDS...

As a young girl I had fantasies of marrying the man of my dreams. We would raise our family together, watch our kids graduate from high school, walk them down the aisle, become grandparents, and rock on the porch holding hands while growing old together. While I admit those are mostly clichés, in some sense it seemed the natural progression of a normal family life. I knew that for our 15th anniversary we'd finally make it to Greece and that we'd give another crack at snorkeling in the ocean on our yearly trip to Cabo, sipping Sammy's tequila. We'd eventually buy our home and paint the walls any color we wanted. We'd both be set in our careers and raise our young son, whom we both adored. Despite the hills and valleys of every marriage, things would be cozy.

However, in that one day, and in one moment, I became a widow at 41 years old. None of those thoughts of "the future" I had imagined would ever get to happen. Poof, all gone.

The clock stopped. My entire life was now touched by Death's hand. He snapped his fingers in a sudden way; and damn, it was final and filled with no-nonsense. That was the day I changed. I was reborn in Venice, Italy. And, I was now on a new journey to "find my independent self." The new me, at least. The "alone" me. The "me" who was no longer married. The "me" without a whole family. The "me" who was not a wife anymore.

My disbelief was still at the stage of, "We're young; this doesn't happen until we've spent our lives growing old with each other." With the weight of the world on my shoulders, I was suddenly responsible for everything. And everything from here on out would be viewed as the line drawn in the sand of "before it happened" and "after it happened."

Everything—financially, emotionally, familial, parental, friend-wise, romantically, and even the way I watched tv—had become different. The joy I took in cooking for my family seemed to diminish. The tickets to go see U2 for our anniversary that were stuck in Dean's email lapsed. The way I eventually wanted to hold hands with someone even turned out different. Every cell in my body seemed to change. Every new way I looked at a situation from here on out would be different than before.

I was a shell of who I had once been; I couldn't even go back to work. My job granted me only three days of bereavement, so I quit. I quit my whole career.

Dean had been the breadwinner for our family and I was always the supplemental earner. I had to start thinking about how—as a single mom—I was suddenly supposed to provide a nice life for me and my son living in L.A., where supposedly it takes a $200,000 yearly income to be happy. I had to take a whole year off of work to recover, to love my son, and to deal with taking someone from living to dead. Getting affairs in order while you're grieving and stressed, all while having a child, two car payments, rent, and funeral expenses was completely overwhelming. But I did it.

I quickly put myself through bartending school to make additional cash to get by. I was spreading myself thin, looking for a new day job, bartending at night, attempting to start my own CPR Training business, being a full-time only parent, and ignoring the grief. I was doing everything to forget. Zander had lost his Daddy, his pal, the one who'd teach him how to drive, shave, vote, play sports, and be a man. How would I, as a woman, raise a proper man? It destroyed me to think that Dean wouldn't be there at graduation, at our son's wedding someday, and as a male role model for him to look up to throughout the rest of his life.

The first year, emotionally, I was a robot. I was still in utter disbelief. *How could this be? We had always been a family.* I was served a death certificate on a silver platter that said,

"This is now your new life." And all of our traditions had now stopped in time and just hung there. I rapidly came to know that all those hopes with my husband, my lover, our family, and our life would never again exist in that way.

Here's one thing a lot of people don't know about grief: Sometimes it doesn't quite hit you immediately. I was scrutinized for being able to smile and welcome people with pleasantries at Dean's funeral. I gave a eulogy without shedding one tear. I even told the story in a proud jovial mood of his dream to open a bagel shop called Rock N' Roll Bagels. What my critics didn't realize was the perpetual state of shock and denial that weaves in and out through the years. I think your brain knows you have to go into "business mode." I had to plan an event. I had to be organized with contacting the funeral home, acquiring the venue for the reception, assigning someone to take care of food purchase, overseeing the centerpieces for the tables, ordering the programs and prayer cards, printing out the directions, blah, blah, blah. Good Lord! It was like planning my wedding again. But this time, it was not a beginning. It was an end.

Robots don't cry. They don't show emotion. They just get the job done and hold it all together. It's not until you hear your song on the radio that plunges the knife of finality into your heart. It's not until you're lying in bed all alone a few months later wondering, "Did this really happen to me? He's really not coming back, is he?" It's not until you remember that summer vacation was coming up and he wouldn't be there to man the grill.

It's the little things. It's like you're the Tin Man and you just got a new heart. But it's the fake ticking clock kind, not your original, feeling one. It's difficult to be trusting, passionate, and to surrender completely. But you go through the motions. No more hand-holding in the movies, kisses on Valentine's Day, cuddling on Christmas morning, or shoulder massages after a hard day. No more knowing looks of "we are in this together." It's gone. There exist only memories and photos from there on out.

It was not until the second year that the widow's fog lifted a bit and I was able to sit with my feelings and be more self-aware with them. Many nights I still fell asleep crying, trying to hide my feelings to be strong for my son, curling up on the floor of my bedroom, bawling in the shower so no one could hear what I believed were ridiculously annoying sobs. I got sick of grief and asked myself sometimes, "When is it gonna be over? When will this feeling of breathlessness end?"

I struggled to go through Dean's things. I didn't want to donate his band shirts; I wanted people to enjoy what he collected. I started sewing them into pillows so people could have art pieces for their couches. I sold them to record companies for their lobbies, to bands for hotel rooms and tour buses, and to music fans. It was a great way to honor Dean and his love for music.

After my 10-year career in ophthalmology, I was ready for a change. Everything else about my life had changed and now I knew my career needed to be different, too. I got a job in the music business and became the director of marketing for a small label. I had a lot of music knowledge and knew a lot of key players in the industry. I always knew that, if given the chance, I could work with vendors and plan events. I knew I'd be great and it was a good reprieve, a lot lighter than the medical field. It was more fun and just what I needed at that point. I could've never planned for a career in music marketing, but as I tried to build a life after losing my husband, I needed to be around a fun group of people.

I knew in my heart that I had to live. After all, I am among the living. But grief isn't something you just "get over." It stays with you forever and touches every aspect of your life. The scar heals ugly. Throughout the next years, I got through each day. I had many happy moments, but I've never been the same since. I have always hoped I may love again while striving to be incredibly independent and make it on my own. My brain has compartmentalized the everyday sadness of the trauma, but that compartment opens from time to time and visits over and over.

In no way will I ever forget what I had. I know what I had, and it was great. It was special. It was heart-consuming. It was a love which I have put on a pedestal. In coming to understand who I was on my own, from here on out I know I didn't want to be that woman who compares my late husband to any man in a new relationship. That "new one" has to stand on its own merit, and I want to experience a beautiful new love in its own right with all of its own intricacies.

But there were so many "firsts" with Dean, which will never be "firsts" again. A first marriage, a first baby, a first love, really. And while I feel I'm honoring what we had, I had to come to the realization that I still have so much love to share with another man someday.

My Pet Grief Dragon

TIME TO GET BACK OUT THERE...

In hindsight, I'll admit it probably wasn't the best time to start dating—right as I was starting to deal with my feelings for the first time; I decided I needed affection again. Nevertheless, as I plunged back into a new career and my "new normal" life, I figured dating was the next transition I needed to move forward.

As humans, I realize we are super resilient. We climb our mountains and are expected to hold our fist up on the top and say, "I made it. I was victorious. I slayed the dragon." But, that grief dragon doesn't go away. He'll always be with me, so I've had to learn to embrace him and live with him—scales, fire, horns, and all.

Why did I decide to date again? Because I'm human. I need touch, lips, arms, connection, and three-dimensional interaction. I wanted to feel known and loved again. I knew there would never be another man to be involved in those earlier life-changing moments of my life so intimately; it would be a different path this time. I had a fear of never experiencing that closeness ever again, while also knowing I'm worth knowing and loving. I think every person re-inserted into the dating scene after years of marriage needs to know there is still a light inside of you that can be cherished and that there's still room for love, growth, and hope for tomorrow.

To be honest, initially I was trying to fill the void I felt when my life and heart felt alone and empty. I knew at the beginning—in some sense—I'd just be testing the waters again. While trying to push that grief dragon away, I found myself as "that" woman who had come to the point of starting over and dating again in her 40s. Isn't that a 20-year-old's game? Where do you even meet anyone? Isn't everyone married and coaching their kids' softball teams by now?

Here's what I found out: a lot of men are divorced and ready to date again, too. But many of these men are damaged as well, and they don't want relationships. They want freedom. That is just something I've had to come to accept. Most men are super busy with their careers so they can pay their alimony and child support, and have 50% custody with only two days during the week and every other weekend carved out which probably won't include you.

In my attempt to get back out there, I entertained organic meetups as well as tried my luck with online dating sites. As difficult as it has been, I truly feel that this has been a completely necessary experience in my human evolvement. I felt like I needed to have these trysts after being in that protective, loving, marriage bubble for 13 years. I needed to develop my "self" again, my strength, a thicker skin to come out of the cave, and to see who and what I really want in my new world. I needed to feel strong and independent again, like a whole new woman because part of me died when my husband died. In the face of death, though, there's always a rebirth.

I was thrust into this whole new world at 41 where I no longer needed to rely on a man, but on myself. I just wanted something new and to be in love again, because that's what I was used to and it felt beautiful there.

I really don't envy anyone who has to be in this new kind of life. There has been hurt, emptiness, and extreme loneliness along this journey. There are men who have put me down, told me I'm gorgeous, said they've loved me, who have been much younger or older than me, who wanted to dominate me, and who are nice but with whom I've felt zero chemistry. There have been "ghosters," bread-crumbers, narcissists, hook-ups, and just plain shallow people who only want sex, casualness, a dinner or weekend date, and never had any intention of incorporating me into their lives. It has truly been a mixed bag of crumbly crackers that hasn't amounted to anything but the fizzle after a firework that has blown out. Some heartaches have even broken me all over again. But it's here that I learned a bit of who I am. I'm not always strong, I make so many mistakes, I'm sometimes too nice, and sometimes I just don't care about anyone but myself.

Yet, I still remain hopeful. I have so much love to offer someone. I need to trust my spirit. It may be that I end up alone in the end, but I can't hope for that. I have to trust that what I have to give will be enough. It is here that I've been tricked and lied to, yet where I've also found companionship and care. I'm not immune to a man professing his love to me and then cutting it off in an insane manner the next day. And I'm no stranger to feeling that "this kind of love can happen twice in a lifetime" because I have convinced myself that I deserve it. And I do.

I've had to grow balls of steel to date in my 40s. I tell myself to have standards now and that I won't accept a lot of B.S. this time because I'm grown and I know myself better, but I sometimes find myself right back there mucking through the mire. I know that not everyone will feel the right kind of chemistry for each person they meet, and I know that there are a lot of men out there who will still tell you anything just to get you into bed. I know that not everyone will check your boxes, and I know that there will be circumstances, deal-breakers, and fears that will always keep a potential love away from you.

After I decided to start dating again, I seem to have had mostly little two- to three-month-long trysts that get killed when my feelings start emerging.

I tried dating while still grieving and here's what I know: You want to be attractive? Then heal. Even now, the grief still creeps up when I'm alone in the car, when I'm sitting at my desk at work, when I'm deep in conversation with a friend and I don't hear their words anymore, when I'm alone at night in bed, or talking to my Mom. Like I said, there's no escaping it.

Dating was awkward enough. Breakups in my 40s were another thing. There have been a lot of closed doors, and I've caused a few myself. Each one, I believe, leads me to something more suited for me in the end. The broken road is the right road to travel here. I am an alive, vibrant, grateful, and positive woman, but I never get used to breakups and I never feel strong right after. There's always that letdown. There's always that feeling of inadequacy and some dev-astation. Another one bites the dust, if you will. I always ask myself, "When will a mutual feeling succeed?"

Dating has not only been frustrating, but it's also been fun! I've had a lot of cool experiences and have gone to places I normally wouldn't have. And, hey, I've been through worse, right? I've had both incredible and horrible experiences here.

At the end of the day, I've learned a lot about myself. I learned I'm not the type to hold too many grudges, so all I can do now is keep my heart full of laughter, keep going, and know I have to let healthy love in to be successful. I think I needed the elation, happiness, egos, mean-spiritedness, and all the misunderstandings to bring me to this point.

This is what has brought me to collect the breakup texts in the diary of my middle-aged dating journey along with their lessons. It is here that I begin with some of the best breakup lines I've ever received. I share a collection of texts because there are very few men who have ever had the courage to approach me with a breakup in person.

This quote about sums it up: "We (men) would rather lose an arm out a city bus window than tell you simply, 'You're not the one.' We are quite sure you will kill us or yourself or both—or even worse, cry and yell at us."

-Greg Behrendt, Liz Tuccillo in *He's Just Not That Into You: The No-Excuses Truth to Understanding Guys*

These are some of the real life experiences, breakups, and lessons I learned from some of my "Misters."

MR. BRIT

first met Mr. Brit during the summer. It was a hot day in August, and I was sitting alone at an outside bar on the Venice Beach Boardwalk sipping a Grey Goose with soda water and lime. A text popped up from a friend.

"Hey, I want you to meet my best friend. He just got divorced." (Red flag.) "Are you open to that?"

Based off of the photo I received, it was an easy "yes." When we met, we ended up really liking each other.

He had just moved in from out of state, and although I was fresh to the dating scene and hopeful too, I truly believe our relationship was the wrong timing for him. He had to find an apartment, a job, and sort out custody. He had a lot on his plate. Then there was me bopping around, vying for more of his time and attention.

We had fun together and shared some tender moments. I was physically drawn to him initially, but as I got to know him, I noticed he was really intelligent which piqued more of my interest. He was quiet and kind of a loner, but I loved that he was a talented guitarist with goals and passions. We bonded over horror movies and Halloween, and I enjoyed doing couples things with him. Sometimes you're just not meant to go along for the ride you're on, though.

"You're ready to fall in love! I work two jobs and I think I'll be holding you back from finding the love that you so richly deserve."

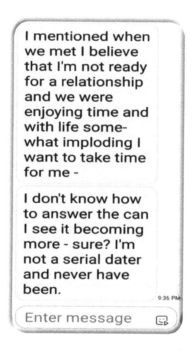

I mentioned when we met I believe that I'm not ready for a relationship and we were enjoying time and with life some-what imploding I want to take time for me -

I don't know how to answer the can I see it becoming more - sure? I'm not a serial dater and never have been.

9:36 PM

Enter message

-Mr. Britt

28

SNAPSHOT

▶ **Best Feature:** Sexy accent.

▶ **Worst Feature:** No PDA—ever!

▶ **Biggest Disappointment:** No Christmas present! I not only got him a funny and thoughtful gift, but I found presents for his daughters as well. Dude couldn't even spring for a card! WTF?!

▶ **Lesson:** I am sweet, thoughtful, and loving. Apparently that's the kiss of death!

MR. ROCKSTAR

Mr. Rockstar invited me and my girlfriend down to a casino for one of his shows. He was the lead guitarist for a popular rock band. A talented musician, with a big, yet sweet southern-style personality and an ego to match. Kryptonite for me.

We were always in and out of each other's orbit as we socialized in the same circles. We had an on-and-off history together for about 3 years. I'll admit, we were friends with benefits and when I was around him, no one else in the world existed. Somewhere along the line, I fell in lust while he fell for someone else.

Loved "Anyways, I wish you nothing but luck!!!"

You're the sweetest
5:10 PM

Apparently someone else is.
5:10 PM

You're the second sweetest
5:11 PM

Douche
5:12 PM

Oh please 5:13 PM

Enter message

"I felt like you wanted a white knight to come rescue you, and I just couldn't be that guy."

-Mr. Rockstar

SNAPSHOT

▶ **Best Feature:** Great hair.

▶ **Worst Feature:** Great hair. Dude spent more time dyeing it and getting ready than I did!

▶ **Biggest Disappointment:** Selfish lover.

▶ **Lesson:** I've had to ask myself why I stayed with him. Admittedly, I had stars in my eyes. He was a rockstar. I felt good on his arm. Everyone wanted his attention and he picked me. But, in reality, he didn't.

*I never said I wanted a relationship. But really, what's wrong with that, even if I did? Oh, by the way, he's in a committed relationship now!

Later, Rico Suave!

MR. ITALIAN

popped my online dating cherry with Mr. Italian. You always remember your first. I invited him to a music event that I was working. And he fit in ooh so smoothly, just like cream cheese. He talked to all the musicians, let me have my space to mingle, and checked in from time to time. He also played guitar—my weakness. I have to say, he did have courage to send me this text. He also took the blame as to why he "ghosted" me. Poor baby, he was just so confused at the weird place he was at in his life! 😉

Listen Teresa, I want to apologize to you for falling out of touch. I feel very badly about how things sort of went down between us. It was like "Merry Christmas" and then radio silence....and that's entirely my fault.

2:12 PM

I really do think that you are a great woman and in all honesty, I was/am really attracted to you. I'm sort of at this weird place in my life where I kind of don't know what I'm doing LOL

2:13 PM

SNAPSHOT

▶ **Best Feature:** Sexy bald head.

▶ **Worst Feature:** Lived with his mother.

▶ **Biggest Disappointment:** We had a fabulous Christmas that led me to believe things were headed in a great direction and then—nothing. I was ghosted.

▶ **Lesson:** I'm a great woman, but some men aren't ready for a real relationship when they get on these dating apps. Why can't dating services screen for that?

▶ **Mr. Italian:** "Don't get me wrong I'm attracted to you and I think you are a great person. It just doesn't feel like the right timing for me."

MR. DISNEY DAD

A loving and heart-felt algorithm on Match.com said we had a 98% compatibility rating. How could they be so wrong? Mr. Disney Dad was handsome, responsible, and had his own home. He also had an interesting, creative career as an animation artist and was a great conversationalist. He won me over right from the start, going overboard with compliments. Incoming love bombs—boom!

We had a smoochy first date, and he was really charming and charismatic. I felt great in his presence and we had such fun times together. Then he called it off. Can you count the number of excuses in this one text? There's at least five!

> I just got out of a meeting where I was told I'm getting sent to Anaheim right now for an emergency repair in the new Star Wars land. I was also informed of a ton a travel I have to do next year. Obviously I can't see you tonight and based on all the time I will be gone next year...maybe we should stop seeing each other before we get really invested and the seperation really hurts. I'm sorry about all of this, it really sucks! I'll call you later 😶

SNAPSHOT

▶ **Best Feature:** Free passes to Disneyland.

▶ **Worst Feature:** We'll get to that. But narcissism rings a bell.

▶ **Biggest Disappointment:** Disneyland for free is just a memory now.

▶ **Lesson:** Trust yourself. You can admire a man's ingenuity, but do not fall for a man because of what he does. Fall for him because of what he does for you.

Why are you on a dating site if you have no time to date,

GOOFY?

MR. GETTY

At this point, I buzzed on over to Bumble where the woman chooses the man. What a false sense of security this gives us! Mr. Getty was a widower, made a lot of money in the medical field, and we had sons of a similar age. I didn't really like this guy. In fact, I was barely attracted to him; but we seemed to have a lot in common so I kept trying. Eventually, he seemed to have picked up on that vibe.

Hey Teresa,
Hope you had a nice weekend . I had some time to think about it and I am feeling more of a friend vibe than a romantic match. I honestly think we owe it to ourselves to explore other options but honestly would love to stay friends.

1:08 PM

SNAPSHOT

▶ **Best Feature:** Six figure income.

▶ **Worst Feature:** Dad jeans...enough said.

▶ **Memorable moment:** He packed the meanest picnic basket I've ever seen!

▶ **Lesson:** If I don't like 'em, why am I dating 'em?!

THE RETURN OF MR. DISNEY DAD

A few months later, Mr. Disney Dad returned like "The Nightmare Before Christmas!" (Why do these men try to ruin my holidays?!) He sent me pictures of his Christmas tree and all the presents underneath saying, "I wish you were here." Honestly, I was single and lonely. That's my excuse for giving him a second chance, and I'm sticking to it. Bottom line is—if he wanted me there, I would've been there.

Second Lesson: Just because you enjoy Fantasyland, doesn't mean you should live there. Focus on *reality*, not the picture they help you paint in your head.

Hi Teresa,
I hope you had a great Christmas! I wanted to be upfront and open with you. I think you are absolutely gorgeous. You have a huge amazing heart and you're very thoughtful. I still feel a disconnect though...like something is missing. I'm not feeling a solid connection and think we should stop seeing each other. I appreciate you being patient with me and I don't want to waste any more of your time. I wish you the best...you deserve it!

Damn, I'm fabulous!

MR. VALENTINE

This guy actually worked for Match.com and sent me a message complimenting me on how perfectly my profile was written. Like a used car salesman, he told me that he looks at profiles all day and that mine was stellar! (Maybe I could write dating profiles for a living.) The only reason I've included this guy is because he had the balls to send me a message breaking it off on Valentine's Day—even when my profile clearly says that holidays mean a lot to me.

9:12 PM, Feb 14

(No subject)

Teresa, wishing you a very happy Valentine's Day, I can tell you're a sweetheart and deserve the best :) I'm so sorry I'm getting back to you so late. Truth is, I was seeing someone for a couple weeks and was dumped for lack of a better word on Monday (the same day we spoke). I just haven't been in the head/heartspace to date again quite yet and just need a break. I hope you understand. Maybe we can keep in touch and perhaps the timing will work better for us down the road.

SNAPSHOT

▶ **Best Feature:** Great goodbye speech.

▶ **Biggest Disappointment:** Breakup timing.

▶ **Lesson:** Even Hallmark holidays are special to me—I like that about myself and I won't change it, even if some of the men I date feel differently.

MR. ANESTHESIOLOGIST

Mr. Anesthesiologist and I ended up sharing a few steamy weekends together. He grew up in the Mormon religion, so I figured he might be sweet and have some good spiritual values. He was adorable, but more than that, he was a doctor. My googly eyes of admiration attack again!

He was on call at the hospital most of the time, which made it difficult to have any set plans. Sometimes I wonder how he fit a woman in, unless it was to just get laid once in a while.

Mr. Anesthesiologist: "I feel that my divorce has had more of an effect on me than I previously thought and it's hard moving forward in this relationship for me."

SNAPSHOT

▶ **Best Feature:** He's the one they call "Dr. Feelgood."

▶ **Worst Feature:** His great career that I admired also kept him busy and unreliable.

▶ **Most Memorable Moment:** The sexy Captain Marvel costume he wore for Halloween.

▶ **Lesson:** Not everyone is willing to make time for you. Keep it moving.

MR. TECH

Mr. Tech was a scientist in aeronautics and wowed me with his savvy and sexy technical talk. I got into a car accident heading toward a date with him once. He brought duct tape, zip ties, and sandpaper right over to the crash site to help me get my car right to drive home. In the end, he used the "busy" card like many others to stop communication and only pop in when he felt like it.

> Hi so I'm sorry that you have that feeling. It's not that I'm not interested I'm just very busy it's kind of the problem that I have I work a lot and had to take care of my son so it doesn't give me much time to interact or date. So I'm sorry about the last couple of days but if you're still open to getting together maybe we can do something in the next couple of days.

Reasonable. But, again, I have to ask: What brings you to a dating site if you don't actually have time to date?

SNAPSHOT

▶ **Best Feature:** MacGyver-caliber fix-it skills.

▶ **Worst Feature:** Never found out.

▶ **Biggest Disappointment:** It all comes down to this—if a guy really likes you, he'll make time for you. End of story.

MR. MILITARY

This guy was a cop who always followed the rules. I was turned on by his assertiveness, which made him very manly to me. To give you an example, he always had me walk on the inside of the sidewalk. He made me feel protected. Unfortunately, he chose another woman with whom he felt he had more in common with in the way of hiking adventures. Which is totally ok with me.

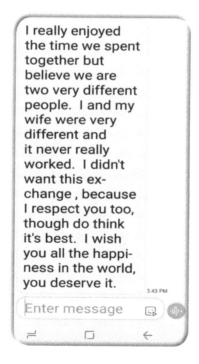

SNAPSHOT

▶ **Best Feature:** Carried handcuffs.

▶ **Worst Feature:** Never used them on me... Meow!

▶ **Lesson:** Most men say that "I deserve the best," which makes me wonder if they have very low opinions of themselves... Or is that just the most overused excuse ever?

MR. DISNEY DAD (YET AGAIN)

M r. Disney Dad reappears shortly mid-spring to tell me how wonderful I am! Ooh, He wants to be friends—with benefits, I'm assuming! Why can't the "benefit" ever turn out to be something cool like a fun tropical getaway? Why does it always have to be no effort and a casual hook up?

> Good morning Teresa. I do know what an amazing woman you are. I'd love to keep you in my life as a great friend if that is something you are ok with.
>
> 9:01 AM

48

DO MEN LOVE BITCHES?

It seems like it's the kiss of death when you're drama-free, exceptional, amazing, and just too damn nice. So many men have told me I deserve the best. I think this is just their nice way of letting someone down, but it's still disappointing and leaves you wondering what their real problem is. Here's an ironic collection of compliments on their way out:

"You're an Exceptional Woman!"

Hey Theresa I can't meet you for a date tomorrow night. I'm really sorry, but I'm just going through some stuff. I'm not entirely sure I'm over my ex-girlfriend, and I'm not ready for a relationship yet. I really like you and I think you're an exceptional woman, so I don't want to let this go any farther and risk hurting your feelings. I also didn't want to ghost you, so I wanted to let you know what was really going on.

"You're amazing and deserve the best!"

I'm so sorry to disappoint you but I have to be honest. I can't say we didn't have a chance, just not right now. Thank you for all the kind words; you're an amazing person also. I totally understand if we can't be friends and I think that's best so not to hurt you anymore. I'm so very glad I met you and got to know you, and I wish you nothing but the best. You're gonna do great thongs both at the new job and in life overall! Take care and again I'm sorry it had to come to this!

"You're the sweetest, kindest, most caring person around!"

(No subject)

Teresa! Sorry, I've been sick the past couple of days. (no corona v) I honestly thought you stopped talking to me as well. When I didn't hear from you I figured you were done. I've had plenty of women do that to me so I just took it at face value. The other part of it is I did meet someone and it seems like we're exclusive. It kinda came out of nowhere as those things do sometimes. I wasn't hearing anything from anyone I was dating and rather than go around explaining myself I just let it lie. You didn't do anything wrong whatsoever. You are the sweetest, kindest, caring person around and I honestly had a great time with you. I'm sorry if I caused any bad feelings, I have just made the habit of letting people do their thing and try not to bother anyone who doesn't want to be bothered. I'm lucky to have met you and I really do value the time we've spent together. ❤

"You're a total catch. My gosh, you're gorgeous!"

> **(No subject)**
>
> Good morning! Thank you for coming out to meet me. My gosh you're gorgeous, and I'm very attracted to you. But I was thinking that beyond that (and Disney, and being parents) we don't have a whole lot in common, and so I don't think we're the match I'm looking for. I am sure a total catch like you will find someone suitable in no time!

...Will the real excuse please stand up?

I think that starting over and spending the energy to know "one guy after another" is one of the biggest struggles I've found in dating. I never wanted to date in my 40s, let alone face the rejection that comes with putting myself out there. It's times like these that really felt frustrating.

MR. DISNEY DAD (THE FINALE)

Ok, here goes my shallow, shitty confession....You're one of the most beautiful women i have ever seen. When you wrote me back I felt like I won the lottery. I love your creative side. You're super talented. The down side is that the tattoos are a big turn off for me and your body is larger than I'm used to. I tried my best to look past it...but I couldn't. I'm an asshole. 😊

At least he got one thing right by the end.
And he had a dad bod!

This ride has now come to a complete stop!

I often wonder what made me keep going back to Mr. Disney Dad so many times. All I can really tell you is that his charming personality and creativity really drew me to him.

When I was little, my Dad built an entire western town in our backyard. He hung old bridles on hay hooks, carved wooden shutters for the little windows, and even let me help him paint the "Saloon" and "Horseshoeing" signs to hang on the facades of the little Knott's Berry Farm style buildings.

Mr. Disney Dad was also building his very own little ship-wrecked town in his backyard reminiscent of the Pirates of the Caribbean. He built a pond, bought a scabby pirate boat, and even designed a working scene complete with a snapping animatronic alligator. I guess I imagined a Fantasyland life helping him make his vision come true while I stood in awe of his abilities, just like I admired my Dad and his talents all those years ago.

Omg, he reminded me of my Dad. Yikes!

Last Lesson: To love myself—mind, BODY, and soul—no matter what any man thinks!

THE SLOW FADE, GHOSTING, AND BLATANT HONESTY

love a good Halloween tale, but what's with this new phenomenon of ghosting? Things are going well, you're talking in a regular rhythm and then—no contact, no response, nothing. Crickets! Sometimes it's a slow fade, and other times abrupt.

Then there's the blatantly honest, which I suppose I prefer to silence. I'd rather know the truth about their intentions, but do you ever wonder if these men think to read their own texts back to themselves before they send them? Here's a small collection:

Another Boy Toy?

> I do have to be honest and upfront and let you know that I'm not looking for anything serious dating wise. Hopefully that doesn't scare you away because you're very much my type 😊 don't want to waste your time if that's a problem though. I hope it's not!
>
> 08:06 AM

This is what's out there.

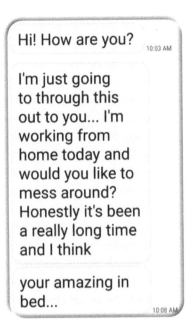

Hi! How are you? 10:03 AM

I'm just going to through this out to you... I'm working from home today and would you like to mess around? Honestly it's been a really long time and I think

your amazing in bed... 10:08 AM

"You're perfect... But I can't date you."

I love you,

you're amazing,

you're perfect,

BUT....

12:30 PM

Enter message

Sooooo Busy

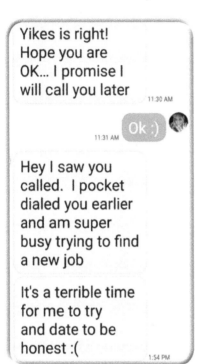

Yikes is right!
Hope you are
OK... I promise I
will call you later

11:30 AM

Ok :)

11:31 AM

Hey I saw you
called. I pocket
dialed you earlier
and am super
busy trying to find
a new job

It's a terrible time
for me to try
and date to be
honest :(

1:54 PM

WTF is this?

Monday, October 21, 2019

J

So are you open
to a physical re-
lationship? I only
have very little
time available.
We can talk and
get to know each
other as well
during our time.
But I don't have
time to go out on
dates and spend
a lot of time. Are
you open to that?
I find you very
attractive....

11:42 PM

"I know what I'm giving up."

I definitely know what I'm giving up. I don't want to hurt you or make you jealous, so maybe it's best we just go our separate ways, sorry. There will be a lot I'll miss, especially the great sex!

9:29 PM

MR. MONEY

This guy showered me with expensive steak dinners, flowers, and bottles of perfume he wanted to smell on me. He bought us matching jerseys so we could attend Angels games together and he even got me a $700 annual pass to Disneyland.

Immediately after, he ghosted me and then eventually sent me this:

(No subject)

Ok, first off, I'm sorry for the radio silence. I literally just walked in my door, I'm home.

I've been in deep thoughts all day trying to figure out what I'm feeling and thinking. You for sure didn't deserve my radio silence and for that I apologize. I've been trying to figure out my brain and why I'm pulling away. The truth is that my checklist you meet them all. And even then some, so I can't figure out why I'm not "feeling" it. Maybe it just comes down to chemistry or some other stupid intangible item. For some reason that I can't explain I'm not feeling it. I wish I could make sense of it, but it wouldn't be fair to you to not say anything or lead you on. I'm not the guy that would ghost or blame a tattoo. However I'm sure I'm going to make your book. It makes no sense to me.... after all you are beautiful, a great kisser, smell great, caring, kind, loving, amazing in bed, great communication, fun, similar interests and a thousand other amazing things about you.... and even writing those out I sound crazy. But I can't deny how I feel. So please forgive my inability to explain or come up with some bullshit (tattoo) excuse. I have no excuse at all. It's just a feeling. I have nothing but gratitude in my heart that I got to meet you. Our one (3day) date was incredible and an absolute joy. Please don't be angry at me. I don't know how to explain. But I would be an asshole to say nothing.

SNAPSHOT

▶ **Best Feature:** BIG, uh... personality.

▶ **Worst Feature:** Duh, dumping me!

▶ **Lesson:** Not gonna lie, this one stung a bit. In the end, I felt bombed with love and false promises. I learned to trust actions over time rather than their words right up front.

"You are the total package, but I'm not ready to be in a relationship where I can't give 100%." I've heard this one before!

MR. RESTRAINING ORDER

First off, I should buy stock in men who work at Disney. There seem to be a lot of them in Burbank. He was magnetic, witty, and handsome. We just "clicked." I would have given him everything. In fact, I believe in some ways I did.

Four years after losing my late husband, I had that "forever feeling" again, like in a fairytale! He even told me he wanted to marry me.

A few months later—without any warning—I got an email telling me not to call, text, or contact him in any way ever again. When I emailed him back asking him why, he accused me of still having an active dating profile and told me I couldn't be trusted. Of course, this wasn't true. We went back and forth a few times and he even threatened me with prison time!

This one shook me to my core. He surgically cut me out of his life in an instant and would not allow any communication at all. I even called the dating site to ask if there was a glitch that made my profile still visible. There wasn't. I kept trying to help him see the truth, and then I realized that I wasn't the mental one here.

In retrospect, there were no red flags visible at the time. I never thought a person could act like that—accuse you and not even call to talk about it. Maybe he had a psychotic break. He had told me he was a sniper in the army when he was young and that he may have had PTSD. Maybe another woman came back into his life or he met someone else and was too much of a coward to face me. I'll never know because the harder I tried to calm him down and have a reasonable conversation, the harsher his threats got.

Nice profile. I don't know why, and don't want to know why. I'm sure you have your reasons. But that doesn't mean I have to accept being lied to.

Do not call me.
Don not text me.
Do not email me.
Do not come to my house.
Do not contact me again, ever.

Other Emails from Mr. Restraining Order:

"Your lies are your problem, not mine. If you contact me, I will file a criminal harassment suit against you. If you come within 500 yards of my residence or place of work, you will be arrested, charged with harassment, stalking, and trespassing. DO NOT CONTACT ME EVER AGAIN."

Note: I've never been arrested or charged with stalking.

SNAPSHOT

- ▶ **Best Feature:** Chemistry.

- ▶ **Worst Feature:** Threatening jail time!

- ▶ **Biggest Lesson:** If it's too good to be true, it probably is.

This "love" took a deep turn for the worst, and I was heartbroken. My friend consoled me and told me something I'll never forget: I bet he's not sitting there crying over you. This helped me finally move on. Why cry over a love that clearly wasn't mutual?

I knew I'd go on again because, without the hope of love, life just ain't as sweet!

MR. DISNEY DAD

Again, ruining my holidays! But I've already nipped this one in the bud.

MR. FRESH (FRESHLY DIVORCED, THAT IS)

had taken a break and it had been a year since the restraining order love. But within the first minute that I met Mr. Fresh, we were dancing, laughing, and kissing. Our spark was lit. The more time we spent together, the more I started to fall for him. I was in my happy place every time we were together. He had so much damn charm and charisma, and every day and night we had together seemed to get better and hotter. I must admit, there were a few huge red flags I chose to deny and I looked the other way. He was recently divorced and had 5,000 Facebook friends—most of them women. He did a good job of explaining why, and I fell for it.

He bombarded me every day with talk of our future together and how much he was falling in love with me. He sent me into a whirlwind. I thought I had met my new Prince Charming after kissing so many frogs for the last five years. Then, one day, he told me that there was another woman he had also been falling in love with.

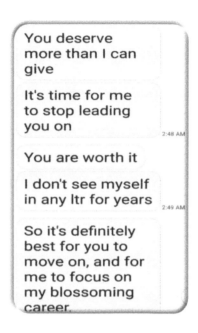

You deserve more than I can give

It's time for me to stop leading you on

2:48 AM

You are worth it

I don't see myself in any ltr for years

2:49 AM

So it's definitely best for you to move on, and for me to focus on my blossoming career.

Because of his recent divorce, he implied he wanted to sow his royal oats and said that he couldn't even think of making any sort of commitment to me at the moment—or for years to come—even though he was "falling in love" with me. Foiled Again!

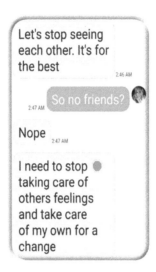

SNAPSHOT

▶ **Best Feature:** Charisma and smile.

▶ **Worst Feature:** Freshly divorced. (Warning: No matter what they say—run!)

▶ **Most Memorable Moment:** The sultry dance class we took together.

▶ **Lesson:** I don't have to seek commitment with every man I like, especially if he can't provide what I'm looking for at the moment. But I did want it with him.

THE ROAD TRAVELED

During this journey, I have cried, screamed, felt angry, guilty, lonely, and lost. I have also felt loved, supported, protected, picked up, and helped. I have opened my heart and soul to new people and have struggled with allowing myself to be happy again. I have been the builder of stone walls while also destroying a lot of those walls and insecurities I used to hold dear. I've become more independent. I've let a lot of little things go. While missing Dean I've handled our finances, our families, our traditions, and our son—all by myself. I value all relationships a lot differently now.

I used to think I could fill the void my husband left by keeping busy or by finding another love. But, no matter who comes into my life in the future, nothing can fill the particular void that was created when I lost him. I have learned that people live with voids, even if our lives and hearts are happy and full. I can look forward to happiness and the excitement of new experiences in my life while still remembering the great moments of a past story.

My marriage taught me that I can endure anything, that I am strong, and that it's ok to feel, have fun, achieve my goals, and try to make connections again. My heart has been forever changed by my experience with death, but it's the way that it's meant to be now. Death cracked me wide open, but eventually I started to mend a lot of my sensibilities back together again.

Most of all, the love I have developed for myself has become stronger, bigger, and greater than any love I will ever experience in my life. In all my searching for someone new, I actually learned to know and love my own heart a little more. I've also learned to trust my intuition and come to the realization that I can, most often, only rely on myself to take care of my own feelings.

I know that in the end, it might only be me, so I have to strive to love myself the most. I have to trust my resilience, my fortitude, all my next steps, and decisions—both good and bad. I have to surround myself with respect, supportive friends, family members, and remind myself not to always be so critical of myself. I need to be reminded to be gentle with myself and the rest of my journey. I need to allow myself to smile, laugh, breathe, and to take the support and love I've received from others and pass it on. That's my purpose in life.

I learn to count my blessings and appreciate the sweet spots. I'm grateful for a beautiful family. I'm thankful for very compassionate, understanding friends who are willing to listen to me, talk through my stories, and lend me advice. I need to be confident in knowing that everything else will fall into place in its own time.

I'm thankful for all the "Misters" who have weaved in and out of my life. I give them gratitude for showing me the patience I've needed to survive my grief. I'm grateful for the love and the distractions so that I didn't have to mourn every moment, and for pushing me to recover and become stronger after they left. I'm glad for the memories we have shared—and for the realization that not everyone is meant to be yours, but there are so many experiences, laughter, and smiles to be had.

Each day I strive to have faith that the Universe puts me in exactly the places and situations I need to be in at the moment. I need to trust that sometimes I'm being protected from something I cannot see yet. I believe that my intuition and trust in myself will never forsake, harm, or let me down and I'll always be ok—even if it takes some time and tears.

If you're centered and believe in yourself, you can't be destroyed. Someone new can only add to the happiness and we will level up together. It's necessary to value everything that's important to you now, because in one moment it can all change. Anything, good or bad, can happen in just a *moment*.

Heart Healing from
Dr. Love Needed

THE HEALING PROCESS

Once I realized it was my responsibility to heal myself, I could believe the door to love would eventually open. Sometimes I feel like I went out searching for a soulmate and ended up with a degree in psychology specializing in male dysfunction syndrome instead.

I've often asked myself, "How do I heal from all these heartbreaks and let-downs?" The truth is, I don't think my heart has been too invested in most of these men. Maybe they weren't really "heartbreaks" but "lessons" I've needed to learn. When you experience something real, it stands the test of time. Many of these men spent very little time in my life in the big picture. Some have taken longer to get over than others. I'm human and each one stung in their own right, but they could never devastate me. The rejections have made my skin a little tougher. They've made me more at peace with recovering.

In love, we take risks. We risk being happy, being broken up with, rejected, divorced, or even having a loved one leave us through death. But what would our world look like if we didn't try to love? We take the risk, hoping that happiness will far outweigh the negatives. Each one is like your own little science experiment where you are figuring out if the mixing of your chemicals with each other will cause homeostasis or a messy explosion!

My life is a cake and everything else is the frosting. You wouldn't put tar on top of a good cake; you top it off with sweetness. Fun, experiences, laughs, likes, and love are all the frosting of my life. The sweetness is knowing how to surround yourself with community, good solid relationships, and people who make you happy. It's taking up new hobbies and doing things you love just because they make you happy. Those are all the things that serve you in life and make it sweeter.

My greatest hope is that I can live a long life. I want to be here for my son for a long time, grow old with him, see my grandchildren, and experience the length of a happy life. Life doesn't come without tragedy or troubles. Life is whole because of the choice you make to live it every single day. Through balance, you gain that wholeness.

To other widows and widowers—the memory of pain might not ever go away, but you are still among the living and you must make an effort to live. The pain is always going to be inside of you and will just become a part of you. In time, you have to have the strength to go on living and make your life wonderful again—despite the pain you may feel.

I like to think I'm running my marathon. I might not be at the finish line yet, but I definitely can enjoy where I'm at in the moment. Can I look forward with adventure and wide eyes instead of keeping my head down and expecting the worst for tomorrow? I believe I can, and I look forward with positive hope and expectations for what will come next.